RAISED BED AND CONTAINER GARDENING FOR BEGINNERS

Kelly Wood

Contents

Introduction

Raised beds can be utilized to grow practically anything. They make excellent veggie planters, can be a charming method to show flowers and are a perfect option for bushes, herbs and fruits. Raised beds can be a gorgeous method to develop prominent planting locations in the garden when appropriately built.

The most practical method to make your garden compost is in an enclosed garden compost tumbler. It takes a couple of months to break down natural scraps into an abundant fertilizer for your plants, so you'll desire to get your homemade garden compost began ASAP.

Get you a raised garden bed and a garden compost tumbler and offer square foot gardening a shot. It's an innovative summer season activity from which you can gain great deals of tasty benefits!

You can construct your own raised garden bed or you can purchase an industrial package. Business raised bed packages are practical because the panels have been pre-measured and they consist of all the required hardware.

As soon as the real estate for the bed is developed, it is filled with soil forming a basic, however efficient planter. If the location where the bed is built has terrible soil quality, outside soil can be utilized.

Raised Garden Bed sets made with plastic panels use some benefits over wood garden beds. A plastic raised garden bed with an interlocking panel style can be put together in less than an hour. The beds in these raised garden sets can be utilized independently or double-stacked to develop extra-deep beds.

Plant spacing in square foot gardening is done on a grid with each square foot including a various type of plant. It is advised to put just one tomato plant per square foot since it is a respected vine plant. For deep-rooted plants, such as carrots or potatoes, you'll desire an extra-deep bed with at least 12 inches of soil.

Now the reality that you've got your unique soil mix consisted of within the walls of this raised bed suggests you will delight in unique and instant benefits that you would not get with conventional row gardening. The soil in this garden bed will never be strolled upon or kneeled upon and for that reason will not end up being compressed. Another benefit to having your plants consisted of in a 4 feet square bed is the truth that you can quickly access any location of your garden from the side of the bed without getting in the garden itself.

As you gain gardening experience, you may decide you need more growing space, especially if you want to start growing more spacehogging crops such as tomatoes or butternut squash, or start a small bed of flowering ornamentals. The beauty of a raised-bed garden is that you can add as many beds as your property allows. You can build an additional bed alongside your existing beds or anyplace in your yard where conditions are favorable for growing. Because raised beds are naturally appealing to the eye, they're a right choice for a garden even in the front yard.

Another aspect of diversity is particularly relevant if you have more than one raised bed. This enables you to concentrate on just one or maybe two crops per raised bed, meaning in turn that you can prepare the compost or infill, to meet the particular demands of that crop. For instance if you are growing carrots or parsnips, then you would make sure that the compost is light and loamy with plenty of sand added to ensure the best crop.

Like-wise for crops like leeks, that needed plenty of well-rotted manure in order to thrive; can be well catered for in their own individual raised bed garden.

As you add beds, you may want to experiment with different sizes and shapes. You could plant a shallow raised bed along a fence and train crops up onto the fence. You might want to build a circular or oval bed, or try a double-decker bed. The possibilities with raised beds are wide open!

Chapter 1 – Why Choose Raised Bed Gardening

There are plenty of reasons why you should engage in Raised Bed Gardening and this includes:

Grow More in Less Space

Because the soil is loose and fertile in a raised bed, you can plant crops closer together than in the traditional row method and expect just as much – if not more – yield. That is excellent news for the urban gardener who is short on space, because you can grow two to three times as much food in raised beds as you can with the row method in the same area.

When planting in a raised bed, you are planting using the 'in row' rather than the 'between rows' method. This means that the planting in a raised bed is much more intensive and makes best use of the area available. This is mainly down to the fact that you do not have all the wasted space in walkways that you have in a traditional garden, in order to care for your plants.

It has been estimated that where a traditional garden wastes up to 68% of the actual ground area. The raised bed system only takes up around 37%. This means that the raised bed is making full use of around 63% of the area available to actually produce something, compared to traditional gardens 32%.

Therefore, a raised bed garden is particularly suited to those with a limited space in which to garden, although not exclusively so, as I will explain.

If you have a larger area to plant in, this is where a raised bed system becomes even more useful. The reason being the walkway around the beds, now serves two beds instead of one for the same planting area. It is merely the 'economy of scale' model in action, where one bed fits in an area 10 x 7 foot. Two beds will fit in an area not double the size, but rather 10 x 12 foot. I'm sure you get the general idea!

It is hard to discuss a raised bed system of growing, without also mentioning – at least in the passing – the concept of Square Foot Gardening. This is a system of gardening, where every crop is grown in an area of one square foot, and whilst this may seem silly if you have not come across it before; it can actually work reasonably well if you get a grasp of the system.

High Soil under All Circumstances

When you build a raised bed, you don't have to worry about how hostile the native soil is to gardening, because you won't be planting in it. Simply spread a base layer of newspaper or cardboard over the ground surface and build up, using enriched purchased topsoil or compost instead.

No Digging

As I mentioned above, if you want to plant straight into the existing soil it is not likely to be very easy to work, or friable. Even if you dared to try not tilling in the amendments, just trying to plant seeds or seedlings would be wrist-breaking work. And if the dirt is that hard for you to work, imagine how stressful it would be for a plant to try to grow its roots down to the level where they can take up the valuable minerals the plant needs to grow and produce a good yield of nutritious food.

If you wanted to be able to successfully garden in the existing soil, you would have to either till in amendments or go through the backbreaking double-dig method to give the soil any amount of friability. And even then, it would not be nearly as easy to work as the soil in a raised bed.

Less Weeding

Planting intensively also has the additional advantage of keeping out weeds. Whatever little space might be left for a weed seed to germinate in, it will probably not have enough light to grow, especially once your crops are half-grown and larger.

One of the chores that I dreaded the most as a child was whacking the weeds with a hoe, but my mother suffered from terrible back problems so I would help her tend to our vegetable garden in the backyard, and this did not only transmit me the love for gardening and farming, but also pushed me to find better more efficient solutions, to make gardening a wholly enjoyable experience. But with raised beds, you don't have to own a hoe. When a weed pops up, and you reach into the bed to pull it out, it slides out like butter off a hot knife.

Fewer Pests and Diseases

When you build a raised bed, you'll most likely utilize intercropping, that means inter-planting different vegetables not only with each other, but with flowers, herbs, and annuals. You won't plant in a row, so the pests will be "confused": in fact, some pests need to land on a particular plant several times before recognizing it as a valuable source of food and if it lands every time on a different plant, it will make it harder for them to target their favorites, they will move on to other plots, and are more likely to be exposed to predators such as parasitic wasps and birds.

More than that, if you use interlining, or companion planting, with herbs and flowers with intense aromas, such as garlic and marigolds you will avoid certain pests all together. For example, sage should be plant with cabbage to keep slugs and moths away, and mint is beneficial against aphids and ants.

Longer Seasons

At the start of the gardening season in spring, the soil is cold and usually wet. Sowing seeds may be an exercise in futility, and digging in soil when it's wet can lead to problems, too — it can ruin soil structure, which is bad both for soil organisms and for plant roots.

For one thing, water drains quickly in the loose, open soil of a raised bed, and drier soil heats up more quickly than wet soil does. And because the bed is raised, spring sunshine has more of a warming effect on it. The bed can absorb heat not only through the top surface but also through the sides. (You can enhance the warming effect by framing a raised bed with stones, which will absorb heat during the day and release it to the soil in the bed at night.)

Accessibility and Flexibility

A raised bed must be one of the most versatile of gardening techniques, because it is so easily modified, and adaptable therefore to a wide range of growing conditions or demands. For instance, with a simple structure applied with one-inch plastic tubing and some clear polythene, you can have a mini-greenhouse in which you can grow fruit or vegetables that may otherwise need a hot-house, depending on where you live.

This same structure can also be used to throw a nylon mesh over for bird or insect protection; if for example your 'greenhouse effect' was only to last you over the cold spells of early springtime. Another good use of the raised bed is to add a framework, enabling you to grow all sorts of climbing plants such as pea or bean crops. You may well say that you can do this with a traditional garden also? This is true; however, it is just that much more comfortable and simpler to build the frame and manage the crop, within a raised bed system

Particularly if like most people you have built the bed out of lumber, then it is a simple matter to attach whatever growing frame you have to the overall structure of the raised bed. If you are care full to attach this frame with screw-nails rather than just ordinary nails, then it is easy to remove this in order to meet your future growing needs, without damaging the frame itself.

Also, a raised bed garden will save your back, which as the years goes; it's an advantage I'm starting to appreciate particularly. You don't have to bend over nearly as far to reach plants in raised beds, which will reduce your back strain. Since you have less potential for pain and much easier access to your plants, you will be able to better enjoy planting, tending, and even harvesting your raised bed garden.

Tip: Make sure that you build your raised bed gardens at least 1 foot tall. If the walls are just below waist level, you can sit on the edge to tend and harvest, which means no bending at all!

On another level; if you have a disability or impairment of any sort that makes it difficult if not impossible for you to tend a garden; then a raised bed system might just make it all possible. Make the lanes between the beds wide enough for a wheelchair – if that is needed, making sure you have a sound level surface to move on, and you are good to go. This system of raised bed gardening has given many wheelchair-bound individuals a whole new lease of life, especially in communities where the local authorities have taken the idea on

board.

Chapter 2 – Site Preparation

O ne of the questions most frequently asked about raised beds for growing vegetables is just how tall they should be. There is no definite answer to this question, I am afraid. There is no 'ideal height'; it is completely up the individual. However, there are certain considerations that you must keep in mind. These include the soil conditions under the beds, the costs involved, the depth of the soil required for your specific crop and of course, which height would allow you to work comfortably in your raised beds. This last aspect should take priority if you are a matured gardener.

Preparation of the Ground

Double Dig

Although the plants in your raised beds will be provided with their own rich soil, some of them may grow roots that extend into the soil underneath the beds to search for additional nutrients and moisture. Therefore, it is important to prepare the soil below by double digging it. This must be done before you start on your raised beds and once done, need not be repeated.

Double digging simply means the depth to which you have to dig up the soil; it is approximately twenty-four inches deep, or in other words, two lengths of the blade of your shovel. Remove all the hard rocks and debris that could obstruct roots from growing down into the ground. Keep your eyes open for other large roots entering into this space. For instance, trees that grow nearby can send their roots to more than fifty feet diagonally underneath the surface searching for nutrients and water. Double digging will provide an extended reservoir of water and nutrients, which your plants' sturdier, deeper roots can have accessed to.

Digging up the ground also allows you to have a closer look at the status of the underlying soil, and to decide which amendments should be made. If it resembles clay, for instance, peat should be used to lighten it in order to aerate it and improve the drainage.

Improving the Subsoil

You have cleared the ground area of debris and rock and finished your double digging. If needed, you can now add some peat moss that will lighten your soil. Because peat has an acidic nature, you have to balance the pH level of the soil by adding lime. Sprinkle some rock phosphate over the plot and mix in with the soil. Your ground area is now ready for the raised plant bed, so assemble the frames and fill up with rich soil. When you almost reach the top of the raised bed, add compost and fertilizer. Do not add the compost and fertilizer too long before the season to avoid early, unexpected spring rainfalls to flush them too far down into your soil.

Ideal Height for Raised Beds

Consider Drainage

Raised beds have an aesthetic appeal, which speaks to many gardeners, but they also allow for proper drainage of the soil in which your veggies will be grown. In general, most raised beds are eleven inches tall, which is equal to that of two 2 by 6 standard boards. (In actual fact the measurements are 1.5 by 5.5 inches.) The reason why this height is most popular is that it provides adequate drainage for the majority of crops. The best results can be achieved if you allow for another twelve inches at least of rich soil underneath your raised bed. That will give your veggie plants up to twenty inches of good soil. Remember that raised beds usually end up not filled to the brim with soil; after every watering the soil will compress somewhat.

You will need this extra space later to add some mulch.

Two factors contribute to the earlier warming up of the soil in raised beds during the spring: Firstly, the soil is always well above the ground level and the second aspect is the good drainage in these beds. Gardeners can therefore start transplanting much earlier and so lengthen the growing season of their veggies. To shield the young, vulnerable seedlings from a late frost or strong winds, place cold frames over the beds. Once the seedlings are stronger and better established, these frames can simply be removed and used elsewhere if needed.

Consider Bending Down

Young gardeners who are fit and energetic might not even waste time thinking about this aspect since going on your knees or bending down to attend to your plants is easy and you take it in your stride.

People who suffer from backache or strain, or those whose mobility have been impaired will need higher raised beds to help lighten their gardening chores. Beds can be in a range of eight to twenty four inches high. You will quickly notice the huge difference between tending these various beds. Taller beds are just so much more comfortable when you have to set in transplants, till the soil, weed and harvest. It is not necessary to put extras strain on your back at all.

Cross Supports for Taller Beds

It is commonsense that taller beds will hold more volume so you have to keep this in mind when you construct a raised bed that is taller than twelve inches, (especially if it is longer than five feet). As mentioned before, after a few watering, the soil will compact slightly, becoming heavier and the pressure may well cause your beds to bulge out on the sides in mid-span. So for beds of this height you will require cross supports. Place them in the middle of the span, right across the width. This will prevent the two sides from bulging out. If you purchased your raised beds from a garden center these supports were probably included in the package but if your raised beds are home-made, you will have to make your own, using composite plastic, aluminum or wood.

Soil Depth for Most Vegetables

The Roots Need Adequate Depth

Most nutrients in garden beds are to be found in the top six inches of the soil. The reason is that most vegetable root growth happens in this shallow depth. The key nutrients like fertilizers and compost are added from the top and then tilled in lightly. Mulches also, are applied on the top surfaces of the beds from time to time; they eventually decompose to add extra nutrients to the soil, enriching it.

If moisture and nutrients are available deeper in the soil, tap roots will grow down to reach them. This brings additional trace minerals to the vegetable plants as well. The larger the plant, the deeper the roots will travel. Deeper roots anchor the plant much firmer into the bed, enabling it to withstand strong winds or heavy rains and saturated soil. Plants with big leaves and shallow root systems like broccoli, cauliflower and Brussels sprouts will need staking to make sure they do not fall over as they develop and reach maturity.

Do some researches before you prepare the raised beds for your upcoming garden since the root depth of different vegetables can vary considerably? This will determine where you plant certain veggies and to what depth the soil needs to be prepared.

Raised beds which have been set on a gravel surface or a concrete patio will not allow roots to grow any deeper down than the depth of the beds. In this case, make sure you know the depth requirements for the different crops. You can compensate for an impenetrable ground surface by making the beds higher, providing enough root space.

The average raised bed is between eight and twelve inches tall, but experienced gardeners have planted in beds with sides exceeding three feet. While these beds are ideal for crops with deep roots, you have to provide good drainage by drilling a number of holes towards the bottom of your beds, right along the sides.

The Height of Mature Vegetables

Tall Plants Blocking Sunlight

Plants are dependent on sunlight for their growth. Plan the layout of your raised garden beds so that they benefit as much as possible from sunlight throughout the day. You have to orientate them in such a way that they will enjoy the maximum amount of sun exposure. Your beds should therefore be arranged to all face in a southerly direction, placing them horizontally one after the next. As the sunlight moves from the east to the west, optimum exposure will be able across all the beds from side to side. Furthermore, this placing will prevent taller plants from blocking the sunlight that their adjacent neighbors need.

I am sure you have seen garden layouts running north-south, in other words, vertically. Some gardeners reason that this arrangement will minimize the possibility of one plant shading another. This may work effectively if you want to grow different varieties of vegetables in the same raised bed. The tallest plants should then be located at the northern side or rear end with the shorter ones in front of them.

No matter how you decide to arrange the raised beds in your garden, it is still important to establish the eventual height of your mature plants to make sure every single one of them will receive the sunlight it needs to flourish and grow to its full potential. In the front or south side, you can plant veggies like radishes and lettuce, following with medium size plants. The tallest vegetable plants will make up the rear or north side of your bed. Remember that those veggies that need trellises like peas and pole beans can easily block out most of the sunlight, so take care where you place them in your bed.

Wind may damage tall plants; their height makes them more vulnerable so they will have to be safely secured to trellises. You will be wise to place them next to a windbreak.

A strong, well-developed root system will provide your plant with the nutrients and moisture it needs to produce the best fruit. If you understand the basic factors about the root systems of your plants; their depth requirements and behavior, you will surely be able to provide them with the ideal conditions for maximum growth and bountiful harvests.

Chapter 3 – Planning Garden

Remember that for all brand-new Raised Bed gardeners, it might be a case of trial and error to the initial calendar year. It may take the time to find just what fits your requirements. There might be failures along the way, yet we invite you to persevere. It'll be worth all of the efforts as your crops will be bountiful as soon as you succeed.

Considering Personal Circumstances

We've arrived at the stage of decision making. Here I would like you to look closer in your situation and the way you're able to determine which Raised Bed system will best fit your lifestyle. I shall break up this with every platform, considering our listing of:

1. Space

2. Budget

3. Expertise

4. Timing

Space

At the start of the novel, I wrote regarding indoor or outside gardening.

In the event you decide to install outdoors, with no encompassing security, your plants are susceptible to pest infestation.

It may be reduced somewhat in case you've got a greenhouse to cultivate your crops. A conventional glass home or a plastic jar tunnel works well. Should you expand your plants inside, then your plants will not be as prone to fleas. Nonetheless, your space might be more limited inside.

If you're considering growing plants that aren't the standard for the climate, you then may either require a greenhouse or grow inside.

In the event you would like to grow from year crops, then they're going to need particular attention to their surroundings.

In the circumstance, you'll have to consider supplying artificial light, heating system and control the humidity. These cannot be installed at the open and has to be under a protective covering, including a greenhouse, or rather, inside.

Budget

The intricacy of the system you've got is also determined by your available budget. You're able to start and ought to start using a tiny, simple method, like Water Staff. As you progress, that is if you will begin to pay more.

You can put all of your gear together by buying each part individually. The only problem you could notice is that you may purchase the incorrect bits and wind up spending more than you initially planned.

You will find readymade kits available with every system. They'll include the specific materials you'll need for this distinct Raised Bed system. At least this way, you may only be purchasing the essential equipment for the job.

Although kits tend to be costlier than the DIY option, in the very long term, this may help you save money.

If you're capable of DIY, then you could have the ability to improvise piping and containers. Or perhaps purchase secondhand pieces and pieces, including a pond pump. You have to wash and disinfect everything entirely before use.

Experience

Whether you would like to develop specialty crops, or even the simpler ones, like lettuces and herbs, then the Secret to development would be to

1. Humidity

2. Water

3. Heater

4. PH degrees

5. Nutritional advantages

Get these appropriate, and you ought to have a bountiful harvest.

In the first seeding to caring to your origins, from light and all of the various methods of measuring amounts, it comes down to the practice. If you're already a keen gardener, then you'll already have a lot of knowledge required in caring for crops. The expertise of Raised Bed gardening will probably come after, with practice and time. You have to consider these factors, however, before determining which system is most appropriate for you.

Time

How long spent on your self-indulgent garden is left up to you.

Decide on a method you know will work on your current timetable and way of life. The busier you're, then the more significant your system. It stands to reason that the plants which you have, the time required. Much like any garden, you'll have to watch over plants. Measuring of varying amounts needs to get carried out. Flushing of systems ought to be carried out regularly.

To assist you in picking, I've gone through every Raised Bed procedure to provide a notion of all of these variables: Space, Budget, Expertise, and Time. I hope that this can allow you to select which Raised Bed system in the event the perfect one for you.

Which System Works Best For You?

DRIP SYSTEM

Space

A fundamental drip process is attainable for any novice. It will occupy a bit more space since there are two big containers. The machine may sit on a desk.

Budget

There's much more equipment to purchase utilizing this technique. You'll have to have at least a circulating pump, a timer, and a tube. You'll also need a trickle manifold. In case the budget is tight, then you can make tiny holes in the machine instead. This system demands a growing medium. It may be expensive to operate than the Water Staff, or even Ebb and Flow, programs. It is because it creates a more efficient utilization of these nutrients, hence using less. This might not make much difference to a bigger garden. To gain from that, you'd require at least 10+ crops from the computer system.

Expertise

It's a bit complex to establish. This procedure is much more complicated than Water Staff, which may be carried out in one bucket. It's also more

Complex compared to Ebb and Flow to establish. If you're just beginning, it may be better to purchase a ready-made kit with all of the ideal elements in 1 area. Be conscious that tubing may get blocked with all the surplus minerals in your nutrient liquid. Be cautious of the since your harvest will dry up and perish from not getting any water. A higher skill level is required for this program. You will need a simple comprehension of balancing the attention of nutrition. Besides, you require a fantastic understanding of how frequently the pump needs to be off and on. Get these incorrect, and your crops will suffer. When it isn't sufficient, then the origins might be stunted, or perhaps worse, and then dry outside. When it's a lot, the roots can clot or develop a parasite. This system is dependent upon electric power. Ensure that you check it occasionally and understand what to do when it goes away.

Time

There are a couple of maintenance jobs that will require focus. The stream of nourishment should be nicely balanced. Verify the pipes frequently so that they do not get blocked. If the electricity cut off, then the entire machine will probably come to a halt. You must check it regularly because it's possible to lose your whole harvest.

Every one of these issues is extremely valuable to the achievement of your backyard. Failure on any of these points, along with your harvest, will perish.

EBB AND FLOW

Space

Much the same in distance requirements into the Drip System, the expanding tray ought to be sitting on a desk using the entire reservoir container beneath so it could make full use of gravity. This program works well inside.

Budget

To put up this system, you'll have to purchase some simple equipment, like a pump, tube, timer, and moderate.

Experience

It's not difficult to keep as soon as you get the hang of this. But, it may be a bit complex to establish. If DIY isn't something, then you will find readymade kits to purchase containing whatever you want?

Assessing temperature and pH levels isn't so crucial for this technique. You still ought to measure these amounts, nevertheless not as frequently.

Time

Nutrient water at the reservoir may require changing every 7-10 days. Additionally, the system will require a thorough wash, with hydrogen peroxide, even following a crop. It's ideal for testing pH levels every day, so it's possible to fix them if desired. You have to inspect regularly the pump is functioning, and the tube doesn't become obstructed.

NUTRIENT FILM TECHNIQUE

Space

The increase tray is generally a gulley or station; therefore, it could be lengthy. Besides, you need room to get a tank that retains the nutrient-enriched H20. Again, it's wise if the increased tray is located on top along with the reservoir beneath. Like most Raised Bed methods, if it's maintained small, it could be installed indoors.

Budget

As it's a constant flow method, you'll require a pump; however, a timer isn't vital. It's an affordable way to begin your Raised Bed growing, yet it's also somewhat complicated, so take note. No medium is demanded. The crops are stored in baskets, at a lid with pockets, so the origins hang out and get to the station of water. To guarantee the reservoir water is ventilated, an air rock fed through an air purification pump is a great option.

Experience

Setting up could be tricky. The increase channels will need to be in an angle so that the water runs from 1 end to another. In case the corner isn't right, then the crops can flood or shut out. You'll have to understand how to measure pH and temperature degrees since these require checking daily.

Time

NFT isn't hard to keep with very little work necessary to keep it functioning well. The tremendous job is substituting the nutrientenriched H20. It has to be performed every two weeks to make sure the crops are adequately fed. Once harvesting, your own body will require a thorough clean outside. The developing station and reservoir may develop with dangerous germs. Suspended roots may grow a long time and limit the circulation of water. If that is the situation, then you can cut them without damaging the crops. It's crucial to maintain the water temperature cool at approximately 68F/20C.

WATER CULTURE

Space

You can begin with as small as the distance necessary to get a 5gallon bucket. Everything which you require can be confined to a single container. It can be complicated if you want to expand the machine after. One bucket, nutrient safety, and a lid with pockets inside are all you want to begin on this Raised Bed system. If you don't develop individual crops in containers, together with all the roots suspended from the water, you then do not even require a developing medium.

Budget

It may be the least costly system to establish. It may run with no moderate by hanging out your crops via a hole cut at a lid. It may be better to utilize little baskets to your roots so that the plants possess some way of support.

You'll have to purchase moderate if you decide to utilize plant pots for every plant.

Unless you're operating a bigger machine, you don't require a water heater.

Should you start small with the entire one container, then you can develop 1-4 plants at precisely the same system. It is precisely what I recommend to the beginner. Start small, and then as you get expertise, expand your own body.

Experience

Water Heater is just one of the most accessible climbing systems. It usually means it is not hard to establish, despite a limited understanding. Plants are rapidly growing within this system since their origins are from the nutrient liquid all of the time. It's not necessary to be worried about studying and selecting the most appropriate medium since it doesn't require any if you would like to keep it smooth.

Chapter 4 – Raised Bed Garden Design Ideas

There are lots of benefits to creating a raised garden bed, as we have discovered. Plants get more oxygen, which is vital to their growth. Also, since you create your own soil mixture you can use the proper mixture for each of your plants, which will yield healthier, larger vegetables and flowers. The basis for a raised garden bed is to elevate it up from the ground, and contain it in walls or other containers. Your only limit is your imagination. Following are some suggestions for your raised bed garden.

Build a Multi-Level Raised Bed

Instead of building rectangle or square beds and putting them beside each other, you can add some visual appeal to your garden by creating a raised garden with several different levels. Build one that's four foot high then one around it that's three foot high in the same shape and diameter. This gives your garden a layered look. You can also build several different large beds and then build some smaller beds in different shapes and sizes. Place the smaller ones on top of the large ones.

Create a Courtyard Using Raised Garden Beds

You can build up your raised garden beds around seating in your yard or garden. Create a beautiful courtyard escape by building the raised beds so that they are tall enough so that the top is just below eye level when you're sitting. Create a single bed or a "u" shaped one surrounding the seating area to conceal it. A stone or block bed can double as seating as well. Make sure that you place bright, beautiful flowers in the beds. If the seating are doubles as a picnic area, you can consider planting produce as well.

Raised Bed Gardens on Slopes

If part of your yard is on a slope, you can utilize the space better with raised garden beds. Build standard beds, and then bricks or blocks to prop up the side of the bed that is on the slope. You should dig out part of the ground under the bricks so that they will be tightly wedged. Then, when you fill it with topsoil, only a little will escape from the bottom of the bed. You can design the raised beds into a stair step way down the slope.

Disadvantages to Raised Bed Gardening

Though raised bed gardening has many advantages, there are also some disadvantages that come with it. The disadvantages include: losing moisture quickly, portability, cost and limits on the equipment you can use.

Moisture Issues

Since raised beds are up off the ground, they tend to lose moisture quickly. Since they are elevated, the soil is exposed to winds that dry it out and it gets more sun, which promotes rapid evaporation of water. They also drain really well, which causes them to lose moisture to the soil under the bed. If you mulch the bed with straw, wood chips, or even plastic, you can reduce the amount of moisture loss from the sun and wind. In addition, you will most likely need to water more frequently in drier, hotter climates to help counteract the loss of water in the raised bed garden.

Circulation of Air

Since the plants are grown more closely together than in a traditional garden, there is a probability that they won't' receive the right amount of air and oxygen. When plants don't get the air they need to survive, they may end up dying because they could end up getting diseases, or they may rot.

Hard to Move

Raised beds are pretty permanent, and therefore if you need to move them it can be a bit of a hassle. It can be quite time-consuming and difficult to take a raised bed apart if you need to move it to a new location or remove it all together. Also, since it is permanent, it can make it difficult to expand or shrink your garden according to your needs. Beds made from stone or bricks are more permanent than those that are made from wood planks. Make sure that you plan carefully before building your bed to reduce the possibility of having to move it later on.

Cost

The cost can be a bit of an issue, depending on the materials that you use for the raised bed garden. If you use low cost materials or recycled materials to construct it, you minimize your cost, but you will still need lots of soil, typically, having to purchase soil makes up the majority of the cost of building a raised bed garden. The majority of the costs of a raised bed garden happen at construction only. Once you have the bed, it takes very little, if any, cost to maintain. You can use purchased or homemade compost to fill the bed and reduce costs somewhat.

If you do have to purchase topsoil, then that will be another cost that you will have to consider. Depending on the size of your raised bed, you may need lots of topsoil or garden soil to fill it. You also will want to consider purchasing some fertilizer to help the plants grow better.

Limitations of Equipment

The fact that the soil in a raised bed is loose and well-aerated is one of the benefits of a raised bed garden. Sadly, the soil quality and the construction of the raised bed garden limit the gardening equipment that can be used to help in the maintenance of the bed. Heavy gardening equipment, such as power tillers, can't be used because they either don't' fit or they can ruin the quality of the soil. raised bed gardens require you to use hand tools instead of power tools to cultivate the soil.

Work

When building and preparing a raised bed garden, you will expend much more effort than if you were preparing a traditional garden. You can hire someone to build it for you or purchase a pre-made one.

Once you have filled it with soil, you can simply start planting.

Plan Well, or Plan to Fail

If you don't take the time to consider the requirements of the plants that you are planting, you will surely fail. You must make sure that you read your seed packages or your plant tags to be sure that you don't group together those plants that have different requirements. You don't want to put those shorter plants that need lots of sunlight with those tall plants that will end up shading them.

Chapter 5 - Types of Water Irrigation System

Garden needs water to grow well. Many people prefer a garden irrigation system to water it themselves. Most people think of only one option, which is the massive irrigation network used in large fields. These sprinklers are usually expensive and hard to install. They can also be complicated. The good news, however, is that smaller irrigation systems are available for personal gardens. They are user-friendly, energy- and water-efficient.

Chapter 5 – Suitable Fruits to Grow in Raised Beds

Raised Bed Gardening can become a lucrative way of sustaining your family with a variety of healthy, fresh food, while at the same time, being an enjoyable and irrefutably uplifting experience.

A wide variety of containers will suffice as growing receptacles as long as the size and spread of the plants are taken into consideration. Often, smaller varieties of vegetables, herbs, fruits, and flowers are preferable for raised bed gardening as these tend to be more successful in smaller areas.

Basic Rules for Raised Bed Gardening

The initial and perhaps one of the most important aspects to consider when planning to cultivate in raised beds and containers is to make sure the plants will be exposed to sufficient light, says Jabbour (2019).

A second consideration is to ensure the raised beds are wellhydrated. Insufficient water leads to retarded growth and multiple problems; least of all will be a poor crop.

Well-draining soil, capable of retaining sufficient nutrients to encourage plant growth, is another important aspect for a successful crop.

Maintaining a steady pH level in the soil is an essential factor for the rewarding cultivation of specific plants, in particular tomatoes.

Composting is yet another major factor that will have long-term benefits for a successful harvest. The introduction of beneficial microbes into your raised bed can have a rewarding effect on plant growth.

Regular feeding with a suitable "liquid organic plant food" is also essential, says Jabbour (2019).

Growing Your Own Fruit

Growing your own food is both satisfying, and gratifying, not to mention a cost-effective way of putting healthy, eco-friendly food on your table.

There is a wide variety of plants to choose from. We will look at the selection of potentially viable fruits best suited for raised bed gardening. These delicious fruit-producing plants include strawberries, blueberries, raspberries, and blackberries.

Strawberries

Generally, all berries are susceptible to insect pests as well as hungry birds. However, if you take this into account when you structure a raised bed for strawberries, for example, you will ensure you have sufficient netting to keep them protected at ground level as well as from above.

Strawberries can be successfully planted through small holes in a sheet of gardening plastic, which is then laid in the raised bed and covered with soil. The plastic sheeting acts as a deterrent to insects that move upwards from the root system and attack the leaves and fruits of the plant.

Light gauze netting is required to cover the entire raised bed to protect the fruit from flying insects and birds.

Strawberries throw out runners that attach into the soil to begin a new plant. These runners can be cut off and replanted in new containers. Thus, a single strawberry plant is sufficient to start with.

Raspberries and Blackberries

Although raspberry and blackberry plants tend to become particularly invasive in a traditional garden, they grow particularly well within the confines of a raised bed where they are easier to control and give a prolific yield.

Bear in mind that if you choose to cultivate these particular berries, the plants will require adequate support for their vines.

Blueberries

Another delicious and much sought-after fruit is the blueberry that grows on a bush. The dwarf variety is perfect for a raised bed garden. Check the best variety for your needs and space (CPC, 2018).

Because blueberries do particularly well in more acidic soil, it is easier to cater to their needs in a smaller, separate raised garden bed. Regular checks on the soil pH will ensure a bumper crop of these tasty, succulent, and healthy fruits.

Cool, Succulent Melons

Certain melon varieties are great for raised beds. Among these are the cantaloupe and honeydew melons. Watermelons may also be a successful choice (CPC, 2018).

Remember, all types of melons need space, as their vines spread for many feet. If you have a sturdy support structure, the smaller varieties may be happy to climb. Melons also require heaps of water, so by keeping these plants well-hydrated, you will ensure an abundant crop.

Take care to manage the vines to avoid them moving in among all your other plants and becoming a tangled mess.

Crunchy Cucumbers

Lindsay Mattison (2019), in her upbeat and informative article, How to Grow Cucumbers: 8 All-Star Tips for Your

Best Crop Yet, gives really great advice on how to grow these juicy fruits.

Like tomatoes, cucumbers are usually grouped with vegetables. However, these botanically considered fruits are a wonderful asset to any raised bed garden.

These juicy, crunchy fruits thrive in well-ventilated soil, and they enjoy good drainage and the containment style of cultivation in a raised bed garden.

Cucumber cultivars are divided into two distinct types:

- Pickling cucumbers, which are often smaller with a rougher, pricklyskin, have a short life span.

- Slicing cucumbers are generally larger and juicier than theirpickling cousins. They have a smooth skin and a longer fruiting period.

You can successfully grow cucumbers from seed. These should be planted in well-draining trays, which will be kept indoors until after the last frost date when they can be transferred to your outdoor raised garden.

Mattison (2019) indicates that within two months of planting, your first cucumbers should be ready for harvesting. These wonderful plants will continue to produce fruit for as long as you keep picking ripe cucumbers off the vines.

Allow the cucumber to reach maturity but take care not to leave them on the vine too long, warns Mattison (2019). Cucumbers that grow too big can become soggy and yellow.

Cucumber vines require warmth and lots of good nutrients as well as compost. Their vines also need to be supported by a sturdy trellis. This will help lift the cucumbers off the soil, thus protecting them from crawling pests. Lifting the cucumbers also encourages better airflow and avoids the development of powdery mildew, says Mattison (2019).

Cucumbers make a great salad and are delicious when served as a chilled soup, which is ideal for hot summer lunches.

Tasty, Tangy Tomatoes

Although tomatoes are often classed as a vegetable, they are, in fact, fruits.

Most tomato varieties thrive in raised beds as they require lots of sunlight in order to produce prolific quantities of fruit.

Tomato plants grow well in rich, well-drained, acidic soil that has a pH of between 6.5 and 6.8.

In order to ensure your success in growing these fruits, be reminded that because tomatoes enjoy warmth, seedlings should only be planted in raised garden beds when the temperature reaches a consistent 60 degrees F, suggests Lucy Mercer (2018) in her informative article, Top Tips for Growing the Best Tomatoes Ever.

Mercer (2018) gives a neat tip for ensuring your tomatoes develop into robust, prolific producers. When transplanting long-stemmed tomato seedlings lay the lower portion of the stem on the soil in the raised bed and cover it with soil. Gently bend the remaining portion upward and secure this area of the stem to a suitably sturdy plant supporter. Because tomato plants shoot roots from the nodes along their stems, these extra roots will secure the plant firmly in the ground.

Tomato plants require lots of good nutrition and water so don't spare the care! Turn in extra compost and keep these 'little gems' well hydrated.

In order to grow sturdy and upright, tomato plants should be wellsupported. Without this, they not only flop into the raised bed, hindering the growth of their fellow plants, but untended tomato plants quickly get out of hand. Decide early on how you plan to support your tomato plants. A cage system may work, or perhaps you may prefer to use individual stakes.

You will also need to regularly cut back all the 'sucker stems,' advises Mercer (2018). This ensures the main plant can focus on fruit production, rather than wasting its resources on side stems.

Zesty Citrus

In her informative article, Growing Citrus in Planters, Cathy Cromwell (n.d.) states you do not have to live in the Sunbelt in order to grow your own citrus. The wide variety of dwarf citrus plants that is available affords most gardeners the chance to cultivate these rewarding plants in their raised bed gardens.

Citrus is not only an attractive evergreen, but the exhilarating and fresh perfume from its delicate flowers will be an asset to your garden. The joy of picking your own citrus fruit is an added bonus to growing these amazing little plants.

According to Cromwell (n.d.), citrus requires a daily dose of a minimum of eight hours of sunshine. Full-spectrum grow-lights can supplement natural sunlight if your citrus is grown indoors.

Varieties of citrus that do well in raised bed gardens include mandarin, grapefruit, lemon, and orange. Cromwell (n.d.) further indicates these dwarf citrus varieties are susceptible to the cold and should, therefore, be brought indoors during the winter months, where the climate is very cold.

In milder climates, plants can be well-covered with a suitable frost protection cloth such as a Garden-Quilt Cover.

Kumquat and lime are the most resilient citrus capable of withstanding temperatures between 20 degrees F and 32 degrees F.

The Correct Soil Mix

A good-quality inorganic planting mix, specially formulated for planters, will be best for your citrus. The percentage of vermiculite is important, as this will allow for good drainage as well as root aeration.

Mix some larger particles, such as wood or pine chips, into the vermiculite to create more air pockets around the roots.

Fine soil and compost are not recommended for citrus as they tend to compact around the roots, thus stifling them.

The Secret to Successful Planting of Citrus

Cromwell (n.d.) says it is important to locate the 'graft union' on the trunk. Remove any shoots below this point and make sure the 'graft union' remains above soil level when you transplant the citrus plant into your raised bed garden.

Feeding and Fertilizing Citrus

The roots of all containerized plants are forced to remain within the confines of their pot. For this reason, it is essential to offer sufficient water and nutrients to the plant in order to ensure its continued growth.

However, overwatering will cause root rot. So, a good rule of thumb is to water sufficiently to ensure the water drains out of the bottom of the pot. You should establish a watering routine where you use a moisture soil meter to gauge the level of hydration around the roots.

Only water the citrus plant when required.

You may find when the weather is particularly warm; your citrus will require water more frequently.

Citrus are generally 'hungry' plants, requiring regular added feeding. Cromwell (n.d.) suggests a good fertilizer that contains phosphorus, potassium, and nitrogen as well as trace elements such as iron, manganese, zinc, and magnesium.

Chapter 6 – Growing Herbs

The practice of growing herbs has been around for many thousands of years, and both medical and culinary uses for these herbs have taken place. Herbs give us fragrances and tastes in these modern days, and they are also a very important part of your kitchen garden.

The great thing about herbs is that you don't have a lot of lands to grow, and, really, a small plot will make several applications for you, and all your herbs for your personal use would be easy to grow.

The best time to plant the herbs is during the spring months, and a wonderful herb garden can also be built in your home, which is attractive and helps to grow ample numbers of herbs. A formal herb garden includes the use of traditional growing techniques, many of which have originated from the ages. A knot garden, for example, lets you grow herbs that boast knotty designs, and this type of growth has been practiced since the middle Ages.

You can also seed part of a flower garden or even a vegetable garden to plant the seeds when you do not have a lot of space for growing herbs. In particular, as this helps to create a wonderful curvature for each floral or vegetable garden, you might wish to grow creeping rosemary and thyme.

The difference between perennial and annual herbs is also significant. The former type can grow year after year and can be incorporated into your herb garden's basic structure. Annuals, on the other hand, must be cleared before the freeze begins to kill them and be shipped during the summer seasons.

Basil is an outstanding example of an annual herb and an essential part of many foods in the Mediterranean. It can easily be planted after its seeds are harvested, but you need to plant seedlings if you want to bloom in summer.

Why grow herbs?

Did you ever buy fresh herbs specifically for a recipe you're about to make at the grocery store? I did. This is an expensive buy, despite the number of herbs that are normally included. They also appear to degrade rapidly, unless careful care is taken to avoid damage.

Then why not go for dry herbs? Well, the fact is nothing beats the fresh kind of thing. Fresh herbs are more aromatic and have more flavors. Having an indoor or outdoor herb garden helps you to easily pick the herbs you need every day and make your home-made meals even more delicious.

Herbs can also have an ever-growing medicine cabinet or a readymade supply of tea for you. They're also loved by pollinators, including bees and butterflies, which means the other plants, will be healthier.

What do you need:

To start with an herb garden, you need a few basics.

- Ground

Whether you plan indoors or outdoors, it doesn't matter, you'll need one, and you'll need a place to plant.

That can be a number, a bed or containers raised up. You have an option, but are sure to check out the Common Errors for guidance on choosing your plants' best growing container.

Most herbs prefer conventional garden soil, but some Mediterranean plants need sandy soil well-drained. That includes the lavender, rosemary and berry. Check what your plants like, and group them together. For example, in a portion of your garden, you can add a small amount of sand to the garden soil for plants like dry plants. You may create a richer mix for those in another region who need more humidity.

- Location, location, location

Most herbs love the sun, so pick a spot to get a generous amount of sun every day. Sunshine is important for healthy development, for at least 6 hours. However, the optimal location can vary, depending on the plant.

Some herbs like it dry, while others prefer a little bit of shade. For details that can help you pick the right location, you can check a seed packet, sticker, or mark on the pot (if you purchased your plant from a nursery)

You can mix tall plants that like to enjoy the sun with short plants that prefer some shade, with a little preparation. A giant parsley plant, for example, may provide shade for low-growing sweet grass.

A significant factor to remember when choosing a location is the distance between that location and your house. Can you face a rainstorm and get some chives for your early jamming? Would you care to stroll to the edge of your garden in search of a basil leaf while dinner is awaiting you?

Some people do not care a thing, but some may prefer to have their own herb garden nearby. Whatever you do, make sure it is easily available so you can keep a close eye on it and constantly harvest an endless supply of delicious spices and medicine.

- Start the herbs inside

Do you have herb seeds to continue inside? You can choose to start planting and choose the "route from scratch," but for beginners, I don't recommend it. The rationale? Many seeds from herbs take a long time to germinate. Starting to grow annual plants and seeing them die in winter is also painful, head into your nearest kindergarten to search for herbs available.

- Plant herbs outside

When you've determined what you're planting, what kind of soil you need, and where to plant it, it's time to start. I like to make a diagram of my landscape, and then plan the grasses I want to put and where taking the height and width of the plants into account.

Instead, it depends on the herbs. In your current soil blend, garden dirt, sand, and/or moss. It is then time to dig. Dig a hole twice the size of your plant's root ball, remove the plant from the pot and loosen the roots. Place the plant in the pit and soil backfill.

Donate plenty of water to the farm. I always think it helps to mark my plants with a clear label on stakes. Often the difference between young plants is difficult to say, so a label makes all the difference.

If they are perennial, the herbs should be planted in the spring, but during the growing season, you can plant annuals almost anytime. I like planting annuals like cilantro regularly every few weeks, so my supply is constant throughout the year.

- Container Gardening

You may also grow the herbs outdoors or indoors in containers. If you need to, it's a perfect way to make sure you can push your plants around, and it can help prevent weeds like mint.

When selecting the container process, be sure to use a container that is wide and deep enough for your mature grass and has plenty of holes at the bottom to allow water to drain out. Put plenty of rocks or pottery pieces in the bottom, so drainage is possible.

For arid herbs, fill the container with compost or sand compost. Plant your grass, and soak it.

- Caring for your herb garden

The rules are straight forward. Herbs mimic any other herb. They need to grow on light, water, and nutrients. When it comes to herbs, there's no special trick. Harvest by gathering or cutting the leaves, as required. Watch for weeds and look out for possible pests before they get into your garden so you can easily get rid of them in the event of an attack.

While herbs in your garden are no harder to grow than tomato plants in your vegetable patch or roses, the problem is that many people prefer to plant different herbs together and treat them as one and the same thing. For this reason, it is so important to decide what your plants like before they are planted together in the soil.

This also refers to providing the plants with nutrients. Be sure to remember your plants prefer the amount of fertilizer and don't assume all herbs want the same amount.

- Herbs For You To Grow in Your Garden

Basil - It is the most frequently cultivated herb and is well known to herbal garden enthusiasts worldwide. The herb Basil grows well in low humidity and moist soil climes. Spring is the ideal season to start growing the Basil plant, but only after all frost risks have been alleviated as this plant is extremely susceptible to cold temperatures and can be harmed if exposed.

It is important to note when planting Basil that each plant is approximately twelve inches apart. This allows the growing plant to access sufficient water and makes it a healthy plant. After the planting of Basil, the development of mature leaves ready for harvest takes around six weeks. When the harvest is carried out, a proper drying method can lead to a savory dried plant, which can be used in a variety of recipes to delight your taste buds.

Dill - Nothing could be easier than to cultivate the delicious Dill herb. Just a dispersion of grains thrown into your grassy garden will lead to stalks that can grow to four feet. The herbal set adds beauty and is used in many recipes. Dills Stalks have distinctive blue-green leaves, feathery and with striking yellow flowers.

The dill plant is a sun-loving plant that ensures a flourishing plant in areas with full exposure to sunlight. The best way to ensure a hardy crop is a gap of 8-10 inches between plants. You will go back about two weeks after sowing the seeds when the herbs exceed 1 inch in height and thin the area around each herb. This cycle ensures that each plant receives the necessary nutrient content from the soil and ensures that each plant is adequately exposed to sunlight.

Lavender - One of Lavender's most natural, fragrant herbs. This aromatic plant is a wonderful covering for any herb or flower garden because it grows delicate pink and purple flowers on high stalks. Lavender is a perennial plant, and in the middle of summer, it is at its best. Lavender is also an essential ingredient in aromatherapy, soap making and potpourri.

Although this hardy herb is easy to grow if choosing to start from seed form can require some extra work. The best way to implement this plant from your local gardening center is through fresh plants or root cuttings. These plants grow well in warm, alkaline-rich soil that is not water-logged. As the winter months close, the elegance of these plants will disappear, but in the next spring and summer seasons, these plants will return stronger and lusher than last.

Chapter 7 - Way to Keep Your Garden Healthy

One of the most mystifying activities that can occur in your yard is when a plant obtains a disease. Just how did it take place? Will it spread out? Will all my plants die? Precisely how can I eliminate it? One of the most vital points to comprehend about condition avoidance is something called the disease triangular (illustration, right).

If anyone of these things is absent, the illness will certainly not take place, so prevention includes knocking senseless at least one side of the triangle. Instead of waiting for a problem to pop up in your yard, think about the best defense versus condition to be a high crime. What follows are ten ways you can remove a minimum of one side of the situation triangular and maintain your plants healthily and balanced.

1. Analyze plants carefully before buying

The most convenient means to limit illness in your yard is to avoid presenting it in the first place. Obtaining a disease with a brand-new plant is not the sort of bonus that any of us desires. Among the hardest points to discover is what a healthy and balanced plant needs to look like, making it hard to understand if the one you want is sick.

It is an excellent idea to collect a couple of books, magazines, as well as magazines that show what a healthy sampling appears like. Do not take home a plant with dead spots, decomposed stems, or bugs. These problems can quickly spread to your healthy plants as well as are often hard to remove when established. Along with examining the tops of plants, always evaluate the origin quality. One does not often see clients doing this in a garden center, yet it needs to be a typical view. Place your hand on the dirt surface with the plant stem between your fingers. Delicately invert the pot as well as drink the plant losses. You might have to tap the edge of the cup against a secure surface area to loosen the origins from the pot.

1. Use completely composted lawn waste

Not all products in a compost heap decompose at the same rate. Some materials might have broken down completely to be placed in the Garden, while others have not. Extensive composting produces high temperatures for extended sizes of time, which kill any kind of microorganisms in the product. Infected plant debris that has not undertaken this procedure will reintroduce potential illness right into your Garden. If you are unsure of the conditions of your compost heap, you must stay clear of using backyard waste as compost under sensitive plants as well as avoid including possibly infected debris in your collection.

1. Keep an eye on your bugs

Insect damages to plants are a lot more than cosmetic. Infections and germs commonly can only get in a plant through some kind of opening, as well as pest damage that provides that. Some insects act as transportation for infections, spreading them from one plant to the following. Aphids are just one of the most common carriers, as well as thrips spread impatiens necrotic place infection, which has ended up being a significant problem for business manufacturers over the past decade. Aster yellows are an illness brought by leafhoppers as well as have a massive variety of host plants. Insect strikes are an additional means to put a plant under stress, rendering it much less most likely to fend off condition.

1. Tidy up in the fall

It is continuously best to clear out the yard in the fall, even if you stay at a moderate temperature and climate. This is an effective deterrent to illness yet likewise an excellent way to regulate disease currently in your Garden.

Diseases can overwinter on dead fallen leaves and also debris and also attack the brand-new fallen leaves as they emerge in springtime. Iris leaf area, daylily fallen leave streak, and even a black area on roses are examples of illness that can be drastically reduced if the dead fallen leaves are removed each loss. If you are leaving stems as well as vegetation to create winter rate of interest, be sure to remove them before brand-new growth begins in springtime.

1. Use the appropriate plant food

You require taking care when feeding plants since way too much of any type of fertilizer can shed roots, decreasing their capability to absorb water. This, in turn, makes the plants much more susceptible to tension from the dry spell, cold, as well as warmth. Plants deprived of nutrients are smaller sized as well as can be severely influenced by leaf spots, while a more vigorous plant can battle diseases. A surplus of a particular nutrient is another means to place tension on a plant.

Obtaining a dirt examination through your local expansion company will certainly supply you with exact info on nutrient degrees in your dirt. Without it, any kind of feeding off your plants is most likely to be guesswork on your component and also might result in too much of one nutrient or not sufficient of one more.

1. Plant disease-resistant varieties

Disease-resistant plants are those that could get ill with a specific problem; however, they will battle the disease. As an example, some tomatoes are coded as "VFN resistant," which implies the tomato range is immune to the fungi Verticillium and also Fusarium and to nematodes.

If you start seeking these codes on flowers, you'll most likely be dissatisfied because condition resistance is hardly ever identified on plant tags. This does not imply that numerous blossom selections are not immune to the disease. Several climbed businesses provide plants that are immune to diseases like powdery mold as well as a black area.

Nursery staff members and fellow garden enthusiasts can aid you in identifying the very best or most free ranges of many plants. Reference books and directories might likewise list plants and selections resistant to particular diseases.

1. Trim harmed limbs at the correct time

Trimming trees and also shrubs in late wintertime is better than waiting till spring. Wounded arm or legs can come to be infected over the winter months, enabling conditions to come to be developed when the plant is inactive. Late-winter trimming stops the state from spreading to new development. Although late-winter storms can trigger further damage, it is still better to trim back a broken arm or leg than ignore it until spring is underway. Always use sharp devices to clean cuts that heal swiftly, and make sure to reduce to healthy and balanced, living tissue.

Chapter 8 – Pests, Prevention and Treatment

Insects are always present in our garden. Many times we think that all can harm our plants, but that is not true. Learn about the most common pest insects in the garden, their characteristics and what you can do to control them.

Aphids

Aphids are a tiny fly, measuring 0.9-3 mm. There are over 4,000 species, but some 250 are considered pests. Its color may be gray, white, red or black, and there are wings in some species. Its mouth apparatus is a sucker, meaning it feeds on the plant's sap. We can find plenty of vegetables, like lettuce, tomato, eggplant, cauliflower, spinach, chili, kale, etc. Aphids transmit diseases, so monitoring our plants is very important. We can find them at the leaves and growth points on the underside.

Red Aphids

To cool them we can add water on the underside of the plants with biodegradable soap, do it really early in the morning or in the afternoon when the sun does not touch the plants anymore. Some natural enemies of aphids are parasitic wasps (Aphelinus abdominals, Aphidius colemani, Aphidius ervi), Catarina (Coccinellidae), lacewing (Chrysoperla carnea), parasitic fly

(Apidoletes sp)

Larvae or caterpillars

There are various forms of larvae in our garden; various sizes and colors. But what exactly is a larva? Larvae are the juvenile stage of some metamorphosis-bearing insects. The larvae which affect our plants come from butterflies or moths of the night.

The larvae can be 1-7 cm in size and can have a black, white, gray, brown color. The larvae are insect chewing and can be located on the underside of the leaves, at the point of growth or in the dirt. They attack most plants in our garden, in this botanical family, in particular broccoli, cauliflower, kale and other plants.

To control them, we can use soap and garlic and chili extract with biodegradable water. Apply very early in the morning or evening when the plants no longer receive the rays of the sun. It's a simple method even to extract them by hand. Some natural larvae enemies are lacewing (Chrysoperla carnea) and the Bt (Bacillus thuringiensis) bacteria.

Whitefly

The whitefly is a small (1mm) powdery white insect. This fly feeds on the sap of the plant, reducing its productivity. A side effect of whitefly is disease transmission. We find it on the underside of the leaves of many plants such as; tomatoes, aubergines, pumpkin, cucumber, flowers such as poinsettia and jamaica, among others. Some natural enemies are the Catarina, lacewing, predatory beetles (Orius sp), parasitic wasps (Encarsia sp). We can also apply soapy water or yellow traps.

Leaf miners

The leaf miner is a small larva that we can find in the leaves of our plants. They make small galleries or paths between the leaves, taking away space for the plant to carry out its photosynthesis. The most effective control is to locate the larva on the leaf and crush it with our fingers, making sure that you do not hurt the plant.

Chapulines

The chapulines are a common pest that can cause a lot of damage since they eat the leaves and, in some cases, the whole plant. These insects can eat any plant. The grasshoppers can be up to 8cm long.

For the control of grasshoppers, we can count on spiders, mantises,

Bacillus thuringiensis (Bt, bacteria) and Beauveria bassiana (fungus).

Red spider

The red spider is a very small insect (0.5mm) that feeds on the sap of plants. Always in a group. These insects form a white spider web on the leaves and stems, thereby protecting themselves from predators. They can attack strawberry, eggplant, squash, tomato, corn, chili, melon, potato, and trees. For its control, an extract of garlic and chili can be applied. If the plant is severely affected, it is best to remove it to avoid spreading to other plants. Good prevention is crop rotation.

Trips

Thrips are small insects that measure between 1-3mm. It is a yellowish-brown or brown color. They feed on the sap of the plant, and they can cause leaf spots and transmit diseases. These insects are attracted to the blue color, and you can put a blue container with water and some soap or sticky traps. Thrips have several natural predators, such as some varieties of mites and the Orius bug (Orius sp).

Mealybugs

Mealybugs are small (6mm) black or grayish in color. They feed on the leaves and stems of plants. Very common behavior in mealybugs is that they curl up to protect themselves, forming a small ball. If our soil is well nourished, it will not be a problem for our garden.

Snails and slugs

Snails and slugs are mollusks that live in humid areas and water reservoirs. They feed on all kinds of plants and can end up destroying the entire garden. We can identify the damage by the traces of mucus that they leave behind. We can prevent the arrival of snails by having our plants in elevated places and using aromatic herbs. Remember they are looking for cool and humid places. For its control, we can use coffee beans, beer traps or eggshells.

Nematodes

Nematodes are small plant parasites found in the soil. Its shape is like an earthworm, and they measure between 0.2-1mm depending on the species. These small individuals feed on the roots of the plants, but there are species that are beneficial (they are biological control for some insects). To control the nematodes in the soil, we can plant garlic cloves, and this will serve as a repellent. It is also important to have a crop rotation and fertilize our soil.

You can find many pests in your garden, but controlling them is not that difficult. Remember to check your garden frequently, once or twice a week. Look well under the leaves, and there you can find many pests and other insects.

Vegetable Gardening Problems – Prevention

There are many alternatives to synthetic insecticides to control some unwanted insects that we commonly call as garden pests. It is first important to know which insects are harmful to plants and which are beneficial, the natural allies of the garden. These allies are very important in preventing pests and diseases as they help to protect the plants against some hungry insects that appear more frequently in the spring. There are still other good practices that must be considered in pest prevention!

How to prevent pests in an organic garden

1. Choose the vegetable varieties most resistant to insects anddiseases. Whenever possible, we should choose seeds from organic or biodynamic agriculture. In addition, it is preferable to produce seedlings for transplanting.

2. Provide shelter for natural enemies of pests, such as predatoryinsects (spiders, ladybugs), bats, birds.

3. Improve the soil structure, adding organic compost or makinggreen manure. As a result, healthy soil will allow healthier plants to grow.

4. Grow aromatic and medicinal herbs to bring beneficial insects tothe garden. In addition, some have a repellent effect on pests.

5. Try to plant in a small space in order to see if there is damagecaused by any present pest. In this way, we understand if there is already a pest installed, and should apply home remedies to control.

6. Cut the first infected plants and remove them from the site. So, byremoving the residues from the infected crops, we will help to interrupt the insect's biological cycles.

7. Take into account the practices of favorable intercropping ofcultures. Consequently, this practice also helps to benefit from more effective management of soil space and nutrients.

8. Always use natural preventive methods, such as biological control.Furthermore, when they are

easily visible, we must collect the pests manually.

9. Avoid monocultures in beds or plots with an area greater than 1 m2. As a result, we promote greater biodiversity, cultivating, for example, some flowering plants such as marigolds, chamomile, capucinhas, among others.

10. Promote crop rotation. Above all, don't grow the same types ofvegetables in the same place every year. We can do a 3-year rotation in 3 sites or a 4-year rotation in 4 plots (more advisable).

Treat a Garden against Pests

Many pests swarm in gardens and attack all plants, whether vegetables, fruit trees or even ornamental plants. Discover how to treat a garden against pests depending on the species you face.

Treat a garden against mealybug

Scale insects generally proliferate on fruit trees from which they suck the sap, causing sores and proliferation of fungi.

To remove them, the use of solutions based on methylated spirits and black soap is necessary. Softer treatment but just as effective: ladybugs, deadly enemies of cochineal.

Fight against aphids

Aphids also suck the sap from plants, slowing their growth. Vectors of viruses and fungi, they readily settle on roses and fruit trees.

Here again, the ladybug can help get rid of the pest, just like nettle manure and repellents (lavender, thyme, mint ...).

Treat plants against snails and slugs

Snails and slugs appreciate the sap of plants and devour their leaves, bulbs, fruits and roots.

The "ramparts" of ash and wood chips installed around the plantations help to slow down these pests. To remove them, there are chemicals based on iron phosphate.

Protect a garden from mites

Some mites (including the red spider) suck the sap from the trees, resulting in desiccation and discoloration of the leaves.

The first bulwark against mites: humidity. Watering the plants well is, therefore, essential. In the case of invasion, there are acaricides, but one can also use the "services" of their predator, Phytoseiulus persimilis.

Treatment against moths

The larvae of the moth (moth) feed on many plants. Leaves, stems, fruits, buds ... are ingested.

Preventive methods to limit egg-laying are essential here: suppress weeds, hoeing, mulching, watering ... If necessary, we will use a phytosanitary product or the Thuringian bacillus (caterpillar killer bacteria).

Treat fruit worm

The codling moth (fruit worm) is a caterpillar that feeds mainly on the flesh of fruits.

To prevent its appearance, there are pheromone traps that limit its fertilization. If necessary, we will spray bacterospeine (natural insecticide) on the affected tree. One can also enshrine spared fruits and destroy those infected.

Chapter 10 - Differences between a Raised Bed and a Greenhouse

A Raised Bed

At the point when the vast majority talks about raised beds for vegetable growing, they mean a bed that has been raised with walls encompassing the soil, in some cases called a garden box or confined bed.

Advantages of Raised Beds

The genius sides make numerous cases for utilizing raised beds. The issue with a significant number of the cases is that they are not contrasting one type with its logical counterpart. At the point when you analyze raised beds, utilizing escalated development to customary cultivating rehearses, you do discover numerous advantages, yet that examination has neither rhyme nor reason. If you need to comprehend the genuine estimation of raised beds, you have to contrast them with serious planting done on level ground, or even raise ground without side walls.

Raised Beds – the Pro Side

There are some real explanations behind utilizing raised beds.

- They require less bowing to take a shot at the

plants, yet a 12-inchwall doesn't help much for us tall people.

- They can be utilized in territories that have exceptionally poor soil,tainted soil, or no soil by any means. Containers are little raised beds.

- They warm up faster in spring, permitting prior planting.

- They can be extraordinary for individuals with a handicap.

- Various beds can hold various kinds of soil permitting you tocoordinate soil to crops.

- Waste can be better in regions with poor seepage yet raised bedscan likewise mess seepage up.

- Bottoms can be screened to keep gophers and voles out.

- It helps shield children and pets from venturing onto plants.

Raised Beds – the Con Side

There are some excellent purposes for not utilizing raised beds.

- You need to purchase soil, except if you have high spots in youryard that you need lower.

- They cost cash to fabricate.

- Soil dries out a lot quicker in summer.

- It requires all the more watering.

- Less reasonable since you have to purchase and transport wallsand soil.

- There is some worry about synthetic substances draining from thematerial used to fabricate the walls.

- Soil gets hotter, which isn't useful for roots, with the exception of inlate winter.

- Perennials should be hardier since a raised bed gets colder up inwinter.

- The columns between beds should be more extensive if you intendto utilize a work cart with taller walls.

- The trickle water system is progressively hard to introduce.

- Soil chills off snappier in fall.

Greenhouse

Greenhouses serves as a shield between nature and what you are growing, and in this way permit growing seasons to be reached out just as conceivably improved. They give cover from abundance cold or warmth just as bugs. While we use it whimsical, the expression "greenhouse effect" concerning our earth is a progressively unpredictable and genuine thought for our worldwide environment, yet for the home cultivator, the impact of a greenhouse on plants can be very positive. The thought behind a particular sort of greenhouse is to make a spot to keep heat. The structure obstructs the progression of thermal energy out, and the daylight that goes through the transparent "walls" of a greenhouse warms up the ground in the greenhouse, which transmits warmth and warms the air. Or on the other hand, if a lot of warmth is an issue, a greenhouse can assist you with making or manage an increasingly mild condition for plants by including a cooling component.

The Pros and Cons

The Benefits of a Greenhouse:

- New greens, vegetable, and organic product

- Transplant accessibility and achievement

- New cut blossoms throughout the entire year

- A warm spot to go in a chilly, dim winter

- Capacity to develop things you wouldn't, in any case, have theoption to develop (fascinating blossoms, tropical organic product)

- No more fights with squirrels and bugs

- Accomplish a greater amount of what you love to do; longer Addexcellence and visual intrigue to a landscape.

The Disadvantages of a Greenhouse:

Chapter 9 – Frequently Asked Questions

Nothing worth its while in life comes free, so we all accept that there will be a little effort involved in setting up the raised beds for our own vegetable garden. However, once that is done and taken care of, you will reap the benefits repeatedly throughout the seasons.

Garden boxes, as it is also called, consist of a frame made from a choice of various materials, which is then placed straight onto the ground in the area you have selected. It is then filled up with soil mixed with a choice of organic matter. Because it is raised above the ground, the frames will keep your garden weed-free and deter many pests. The frames also prevent soil erosion and soil compaction. It offers excellent drainage and saves space.

The experience of gardeners is that raised beds are super productive and extremely convenient. I will now address some of the frequently asked questions about how to go about when you start your own vegetable plants in garden boxes.

1.Why consider raised beds for my vegetable garden?

If you are a very busy person with little free time, this is for you. It takes a lot less time managing raised beds than it would a complete garden plot and it is in fact a lot easier. If your gardening space is limited, the soil in your garden is of a poor quality or even if there is an area in your existing garden that is a real eyesore, raised beds can solve all your problems. Many gardeners find that raised beds give their vegetable gardens a neater and tidier look and that these beds produce quite a bit more veggies.

2.When is a good time to set up the raised beds?

You can start anytime you want so do not postpone it too long. They have to be ready when the growing season starts so I would suggest setting it up in the early spring.

3.How big should my raised beds be?

You determine the size of your beds as long as they fit the available space, of course. The general rule is not to make them wider than four feet along one side. You will find that this width allows you easy access from all sides for your weeding, cultivating, and harvesting. Anything wider and you might find yourself stretching to reach all the different areas of your beds.

How high you decide to make your beds is also your choice. Disabled or elderly gardeners should carefully consider which height would be convenient for them; usually it should be the height of your waist. This makes it easy to sit in the sides while you do your maintenance and prevent you from having to bend down too much.

4.If I am not a handy person how can I make a raised bed?

You do not have to construct your own beds from scratch. Many garden centers sell ready-made ones or frames that are very simple to assemble yourself. Just follow the instructions, they will show you how to do it one-step at a time. The fact is that these beds can be constructed from a number of different materials, like metal, wood, plastic or even cinder blocks.

5.Is it necessary to prepare the soil under my raised bed?

Although it is not a hard and fast rule, I would strongly recommend that you do it. If you loosen this soil and get rid of all the debris and rocks, the roots of your plants can reach down deeper into the soil for the nutrients and water they need. This will mean a stronger and healthier root system that in turn will ensure plants that are more productive.

This may sound like a lot of extra work, but you need to do it only once – right in the beginning before you assemble your bed. Dig down to around twenty-four inches of the surface, adding humus, topsoil, compost and some extra organic matter. The soil underneath your bed should be similar to the soil in your raised bed.

6.How many vegetable plants can I grow in my raised bed?

It depends on the type of plants you want to grow. In a four by four bed, you will be able to accommodate up to six low growing vegetable plants, for instance squash, cucumbers, zucchini and herbs. Plant a few of the taller vegetables in the very center of your bed; tomatoes would work well. If you have a longer bed, say around eight feet, you can set up one or two trellises for your vining crops.

Beans or peas will do well.

7.Which should I plant – seedlings or seeds?

The rules are the exact same as you would follow when you plan your vegetables in plots in the garden. Some crops will do better if you start with seedlings. These include perennial herbs, peppers and tomatoes. Others will be more successful if you sow the seeds straight into the raised beds. These include lettuces, beans, radishes, cucumbers, squash and basil.

8.What is the best way to water my vegetables in raised beds?

You can always do it manually but take care when you water young tender seedlings that you do not damage them or wash away the soil around them. A drip irrigation system would be ideal since it regulates the amount of water your plants receive while providing the moisture in the correct doses.

Conclusion

Raised beds are growing in popularity for all levels of gardeners. Regardless of whether you are a specialist, novice, senior resident or even a kid, you can find how simple and advantageous it is to plant with a superb planter bed.

Beginner's need to set up a great deal of things for building up a new garden behind your home; it can likewise provide you with a lot of fun. If it is the first time you will going to develop a garden you should have a small one at first and afterward you can grow it in the later season which likewise comprises of vegetable gardens for beginners, vegetable gardening for beginners.

When you raise the bed of your planting surface you achieve a few things. Getting a planting surface lifted for a senior citizen is often the difference of them making the most of their lifelong quest for flowers or vegetable planting. This is likewise regularly helpful in mitigating back and neck strain that can get intolerable in older individuals.

By raising the grower to eye level and a safe distance you are carrying the nursery to where it is agreeable for you. For kids and even learner nursery workers, lifting the bed considers a controlled area that is easily maintained. Rather than having an overwhelming area that can quickly get out of control, you have a smaller space that requires less weeding and pruning. Expert gardeners love the common sense of raised bed cultivating. At the point when the depth of the territory is extended by lifting it, you create an environment where the soil remains loose and deep, rather than compacted.

Plants prefer this kind of condition and will prosper by having the option to sink its roots deep into the ground. Also, many planting beds are being made of reused materials and wooden materials that are resistant to insects. This makes organic gardening a realistic possibility at your home no matter that your skill level.

So there you have it. Everything you wanted to know about getting into raised bed gardens is now in your hand. It is my hope that this book has helped to answer many of the questions you had about starting your own raised bed garden. From why you would want to start one through to how it's done and how it is maintained, my goal has been to give you the information you need to get started. But that has only been half of my goal.

Giving you the information you need to get started is important but I have tried my best to stress the importance of researching your plants and listening to your garden. Taking the time to spend a few minutes every day with your garden will let you gather in firsthand experience what you would learn from a year of studying. Reading how it is done in a book is one thing but actually getting your hands dirty and learning to listen to your plants will take time and effort. It might sound like a lot of work but once you get into a flow of things, it is easy to lose track of how much time you are spending in your garden. It becomes such a peaceful hobby.

But it is also so rewarding. Watching the way your plants grow and thrive due to the careful consideration you have taken in setting up their raised bed home is a truly magical experience. Whether you are growing for beauty, consumption, or profit, you will find that the best part of the whole project is spending time with your plants and learning how they grow and communicate with us, their environment, and each other.

I hope that this book has left you with plenty of new questions and lots of ideas for how you could create wonderful raised bed gardens of your own. Make sure you take lots of photos to share the beautiful designs you've come up with so that you can inspire others to take up raised bed gardening themselves.

CPSIA information can be obtained
at www.ICGtesting.com
Printed in the USA
LVHW052009150623
749904LV00006B/79